Contents

Context

Outliers, originally published in 2008, speaks to a culture that regards success largely as a product of individual exceptionalism. It was written at a time when the growth of the tech industry saw the meteoric rise of young moguls such as Mark Zuckerberg, who took Facebook from a dorm-room lark to a multibillion-dollar business—and transformative societal force—seemingly overnight. The popular perception of Zuckerberg and others as visionary prodigies who found fortune and fame through sheer ingenuity is the sort of oversimplified origin narrative that Gladwell is seeking to debunk with his alternative perspective on outliers.

In our current age of ever-increasing polarization of wealth and fetishization of fame, the lessons of *Outliers* may prove very instructive. The idea that there is no such thing as a purely self-created success story may help us to think of ways to increase opportunities for the many and not just the few.

Overview

The secret of success is something many of us spend our lives seeking. But what if we've been looking in the wrong places all along? We often assume that those who are successful beyond our wildest dreams—think of Bill Gates or the members of the Beatles—must possess some preternatural genius that unequivocally sets them apart from average folks. But Malcolm Gladwell makes a compelling argument in *Outliers* that, while exceptional ability is certainly a factor in success, it's not the defining one. Instead, he argues—citing a series of fascinating statistics and entertaining anecdotes—that success is largely a product of fortuitous opportunities, diligent work, and the circumstances in which we are born, brought up, and nurtured. After all, what use is talent if it isn't cultivated and put into practice?

Summary

Introduction: The Roseto Mystery

The insular town of Roseto, Pennsylvania, populated by descendants of Italian immigrants from Roseto Valfortore, Italy, is a curious medical anomaly: As early as the 1950s, the rate of heart disease and other ailments there was shockingly lower than the rest of the United States. Societal ills such as substance abuse and crime were also strikingly scarce. So what set Roseto apart? As physician Stewart Wolf discovered, the obvious potential causes—a healthy lifestyle, diet, genetics, and so forth—didn't seem to be in play. Instead, he concluded that the distinctive sense of community in the self-contained town—for instance, neighbors greeting one another, multiple generations of a family sharing a home, an overall "egalitarian ethos"—had a positive effect on the population's health and quality of life. Gladwell frames this surprising, paradigm-shifting lesson about health as an analogy for the argument *Outliers* will make about success.

Need to Know: Health may not be entirely about an individual's constitution or life choices—it has a lot to do with the cultural context in which a person lives. And that same principle may apply to personal success.

Chapter One: The Matthew Effect

We're accustomed to thinking of success as the result of some special, almost magical talent that allows individuals to shine and overcome any obstacles in their path, no matter what advantages they have or haven't been given. (Think of the classic "pulled himself up by his bootstraps" narrative.) But Gladwell is making the case that we *are* affected by the circumstances we're born into and the happy (or unhappy) situations we encounter along our lives.

To wit: An astounding number of Canada's elite junior hockey players were born in January, followed by February and March. This phenomenon can be explained by the fact that the age cutoff for youth hockey is January 1—so boys born in January could be playing with kids almost a year younger, which almost guarantees that the older players will stand out as having better ability. As coaches winnow down their teams to their perceived "all-stars," these older boys are more likely to be selected for the elite squads . . . and hence to receive an advanced level of training and increased practice opportunities that help them develop their abilities and—literally—skate to success. (This phenomenon is also observed in other age-eligibility-limited sports, such as soccer.)

Need to Know: The "Matthew effect"—so called for the Biblical verse Matthew 25:29, which says that those with advantages will be given more, while those without will have theirs taken away—is a kind of snowball effect. An arbitrary advantage (such as one's date of birth relative to competitors) may well be rewarded with further opportunities, which reinforce the perception of superior ability and lead to ever more opportunities . . . and so the achievement gap just keeps widening.

Chapter Two: The 10,000-Hour Rule

What does it take to turn talent and drive into success? We might think the answer lies in some ineffable quality or stroke of fate. Turns out, it can be quantified: by at least 10,000 hours spent practicing and honing one's gifts. And often, getting the chance to log those 10,000 hours of focused effort hinges on being in the right place at the right time.

Some striking examples: Bill Joy, cofounder of Sun Microsystems and widely considered to be a groundbreaker in modern computing, had the good fortune to attend the University of Michigan, where a then practically one-of-a-kind computer center became his second home. Mozart is often cited as a prodigy for composing concertos starting at age 6—but his work didn't reach masterpiece level until he was 21. By the time of their American "Invasion," the Beatles had honed their talents performing hundreds of marathon gigs in Hamburg, Germany, sometimes clocking eight hours at a stretch.

And finally, one of the ultimate outliers, Microsoft cofounder Bill Gates, had the stunning good luck to start seventh grade at a private school with a computer club funded by students' parents—a resource that the vast majority of college students didn't have at the time. Gates was one of a generation of tech pioneers born in or around 1955, a demographic sweet spot for nerds due to the transformational innovations in technology that were taking place as they came of age.

Need to Know: Malcolm Gladwell isn't denying that innate talent plays a part in success—who would argue that Mozart, the Beatles, or Bill Gates weren't gifted with anything more than practice time? But he does note that 10,000-hours is a fairly reliable benchmark for how long it takes a person to master their craft, if one is capable of and driven toward that level of mastery.

Chapter Three: The Trouble With Geniuses, Part 1

Does a superior intellect always pan out into superior achievement? We'd like to think that true genius always shines through, like a diamond in the rough. But evidence suggests that transcendental brainpower can't necessarily overcome the obstacles one is born facing—and in a bigger picture of success, pure intelligence is just one piece of the puzzle.

Chris Langan, described by Gladwell as "the public face of genius in American life, a celebrity outlier," has an IQ that is "literally off the charts"—too high to be accurately measured by standard testing—but never achieved true "outlier" status. Gladwell argues, citing psychologist Liam Hudson, that there's a certain upper threshold beyond which additional IQ points don't count for much in terms of predicting achievement, such as the Nobel Prize. (Consider the analogy of basketball—height matters up to a point, but doesn't necessarily correlate with skill once you're looking at the difference between, say, six foot eight and six foot six.)

The "threshold effect"—the idea that past a certain point, additional IQ points don't mean much—suggests that other factors come into play in determining success potential. Gladwell cites an example of a "divergence test," which, as opposed to a "convergence test" such as the standard IQ test, has no correct answers to arrive at, instead inviting the taker to come up with responses. Pure analytical intelligence, as measured in IQ points, won't give you the creativity and imagination to open your mind to unconventional responses—what we might call thinking outside the box.

One story that illustrates this point: In the 1920s, Lewis Terman, a Stanford psychology professor, embarked on a longitudinal study of children identified as possessing extraordinarily high IQs, anticipating that they would go on to accomplish great things. But this cadre of Terman's "Termites," as they came to be known, did not grow up to achieve the kind of distinction one might expect from beyond-99th-percentile intellects. While some found moderate success, none became true luminaries. Gladwell contends that Terman was myopic in focusing purely on IQ as a predictor of achievement.

Need to Know: The idea that when it comes to IQ, the "cream of the crop" will always float to the top is a common misconception. While a certain level of intelligence may be a prerequisite for success, additional IQ points past that threshold may not make much of a difference. Other variables, such as imagination, are necessary to really make people shine.

Chapter Four: The Trouble With Geniuses, Part 2

The life story of Chris Langan is indeed, as Gladwell says, "heartbreaking." Raised in a poor family with an abusive stepfather in Bozeman, Montana, he enrolled in Oregon's Reed College on a full scholarship, but lost it when his mother failed to fill out the renewal forms. After dropping out of Montana State University, he worked in construction, on a clam boat, and as a bouncer . . . all while reading scholarly texts and penning a work he calls the "Cognitive Theoretical Model of the Universe." He now resides on a horse farm in Missouri, while continuing his own learning independently. Langan is an off-the-charts genius, but he never had any support, and he never caught a break, and he didn't possess the social savvy for sweet-talking—say, the dean at Reed—into giving him one.

By contrast, Robert Oppenheimer, the father of the atomic bomb, had genius, means, and "practical intelligence"—the sort of savvy that leads you intuitively to say the right thing to the right person at the right time, which Langan lacked. Granted, Langan's upbringing did not exactly lend itself to the development of social skills, while Oppenheimer was raised in an environment of support and encouragement—plus a privileged background complete with summer trips to Europe—that cultivated them. He landed the plum role of scientific director of the Manhattan Project at age 38—despite the fact that in grad school, he had attempted to poison his tutor with lab chemicals. (Apparently, Oppenheimer was angry at the tutor for making him study a branch of physics he didn't enjoy.)

Upbringing may play a vital role in determining whether talent will lead to success. Sociologist Annette Lareau, who intensively studied third-graders from rich and poor households, shadowing their families throughout their daily routines, found that the well-to-do parents were deeply invested in their children's highly scheduled activities, and gave them a sense of "entitlement"—the impression that their opinions and preferences mattered, and that they should feel comfortable speaking up to get what they wanted. On the other hand, the parents of poor kids largely left them to their own devices, and the intimidation they often felt around authority figures was passed on to their children. This group of kids experienced "constriction"—the opposite of entitlement. They didn't have the confidence to assert themselves.

Perhaps unsurprisingly, Terman's findings about his "Termites"—whom he divided into A, B, and C groups based on their level of academic and professional achievement—aligned neatly along lines of "family background." Those who had graduated from college and found professional success (the 150 "As") came primarily from educated families who had encouraged them, while the 150 "Cs" who struggled even to make a living were, as Gladwell puts it, "from the other side of the tracks."

Need to Know: When it comes to career achievement, intellectual superiority may not be much of an advantage if it isn't accompanied by social skills and social privilege—and those social skills seem often to stem from that privilege.

Chapter Five: The Three Lessons of Joe Flom

Joe Flom was a Jewish lawyer who cut his teeth in the 1950s and '60s on the kind of litigation that the WASPy "white-shoe" law firms wouldn't touch back in the day, and eventually became a named partner in the renowned multibillion-dollar firm now known as Skadden, Arps, Slate, Meagher & Flom LLP. As Gladwell tells it, being the child of poor immigrants from Eastern Europe would seem like a disadvantage when trying to break into the elitist and somewhat anti-Semitic world of law at that time—but Flom actually benefited from certain factors that helped make him an outlier.

First, the fact that the "old-line law firms" refused to get their hands dirty with legal actions like hostile takeovers—considered unseemly until the 1970s—allowed Flom and others like him to master that niche. And by the time such Wall Street maneuvers became big business in the '70s and '80s, they had built their reputations as the go-to guys for that kind of wheeling and dealing.

Secondly, Flom was born in a demographic sweet spot—1930—much like Bill Gates's generation of tech moguls. As the US birthrate had dipped due to the Great Depression, men of Flom's age faced less competition for college admissions and job openings. And thirdly, though his father and many other immigrants of his generation had toiled long hours for little profit in the garment industry, their example had established the value of hard but "meaningful" work in a skilled trade they had learned in the Old World. Through their grueling labor—combined with skill, ingenuity, and creativity—these tradesmen passed down to their children the idea that work with "autonomy, complexity, and a connection between effort and reward" is satisfying and meaningful. Strikingly, many of these immigrants had offspring who went on to become doctors or lawyers.

Need to Know: The dedicated and skilled labor of a wave of European immigrant tradespeople, plus a fortuitous "demographic trough" of low birthrate, produced a generation of high achievers among their offspring. And their lesson, to their children and the rest of us, is that willingness to devote boundless time and energy to creative, challenging, and autonomous work leads to job satisfaction and the potential for great success.

Chapter Six: Harlan, Kentucky

We've all heard the notorious story of the Hatfield-McCoy family feud. But it turns out that there are plenty of other instances of warfare between rival clans in the Appalachians in the nineteenth century. One such conflict is that of the Howards and Turners in Harlan County, Kentucky. The families traded gunfire on repeated occasions, and the casualties mounted on both sides—the violence becoming so commonplace that Mrs. Turner scolded her dying son to stop moaning and groaning over his gunshot wounds: "Die like a man, like your brother did!"

These sorts of family feuds were common in Appalachia because of a particular convergence of factors: The area's residents were descendants of a Scotch-Irish "culture of honor" in which slights were to be avenged, not forgiven. And as in the highlands of their ancestral homelands, the prevailing livelihood was herding, not farming—a line of work that requires vigilance against animal thieves, and the ability to intimidate as a deterrent.

This honor culture persists in the South to this day, as evidenced by a modern University of Michigan study in which student subjects were provoked by being called "asshole." The Northerners didn't get too worked up about it, while the Southerners—a well-educated, affluent lot, mind you—displayed signs of anger, including increased testosterone and cortisol levels.

Need to Know: Long after the direct circumstances that shape cultural legacies cease to be in play, their effects continue to shape characteristics of a society. Evidence shows that traits passed on from long-gone ancestors exert a strong influence on their modern-day descendants.

Chapter Seven: The Ethnic Theory of Plane Crashes

If cultural heritage has such a profound influence on individuals, could it actually play a role in events such as plane crashes? Two examples—the Korean Air Flight 801 crash in 1997 in Guam and Avianca Flight 052 in New York in 1990—suggest the answer is yes. In both cases, the crashes were not caused by mechanical error of the aircraft. Rather, an incremental series of human errors were compounded, black box recorder transcripts indicate, by poor communication. And those failures of communication were, in turn, caused by a culturally ingrained deference to authority.

In the Korean Air tragedy, the captain, fatigued from a long shift of flying, attempted to land, guided only by eyesight in stormy conditions. He made a fatal miscalculation that missed the runway by miles and sent the plane into the side of a hill. His first officer, accustomed to accepting the higher-ranking pilot's authority without question, made a tentative suggestion that weather radar might be useful, but didn't push it.

On the Avianca flight, the Colombian crew had been circling JFK so long, the plane was running out of fuel, but the first officer failed to forcefully convey that fact to the notoriously intimidating New York airport's Air Traffic Control. The plane ultimately crashed and burned in Long Island.

What's telling about these two incidents is that both Korean and Colombian cultures have what is called a high "power distance index"—a regard for rank and authority so deeply ingrained that the barrier for a subordinate to speak up to a superior is practically insurmountable. This is conducive to "mitigated speech," a form of indirect communication that requires the listener to read (or rather, hear) between the lines. While Western culture's communications have a "transmitter orientation"—placing the burden of getting the message across on the one conveying it—Korean culture is "receiver oriented," meaning it's on you to get the message.

Korean Air was able to recover from its poor safety record, Gladwell notes, by hiring a consultant from Delta Airlines who mandated that all pilots must speak English. By changing their communication patterns, crews were able to dispense with some of the cultural conventions that could inhibit them from collaborating effectively.

Need to Know: Plane crashes in the modern age tend to be "the result of an accumulation of minor difficulties and seemingly trivial malfunctions," often brought about by poor weather conditions and pilot fatigue, rather than some catastrophic mechanical failure of the aircraft. And flight crews from relatively egalitarian cultures that have a low "power distance index" may be better equipped to avert these tragedies, since subordinates will more readily speak up to their superiors in a moment of crisis.

Chapter Eight: Rice Paddies and Math Tests

So far we've learned of some surprising ways that cultural heritage comes into play—from anger triggers to plane crashes—but there are still more ways that culture unconsciously plays a role in success. It turns out that the complexity and diligence involved in cultivating rice paddies might well relate to the much-vaunted (or much-stereotyped) ability of Asians to excel in math. Requisites for this very precise agricultural art, such as an intricate irrigation system, precise fertilizer blending and application, and selection of the right rice varietal (among other painstaking tasks), require tremendous commitment and concentration—skills that could also come in handy for solving math problems.

The Chinese language is structured with short and consistent words for numbers, giving its speakers an advantage over native English speakers in terms of learning basic calculation skills and memorizing numerical sequences. Thus, students may be less likely to get frustrated with the subject, and more motivated to actually enjoy it. But also, the cultural legacy of a society that revolved around rice paddy agriculture—developing diligence, industriousness, and problem-solving ability—might have helped foster the propensity for math skills.

Need to Know: Perseverance in problem-solving—the ability to work toward a desired result, when a less dedicated person might likely throw up his or her hands and give up—was a hallmark of the Chinese culture of rice paddy farming, and is an indicator of agility with math—and not just among the Chinese. In fact, an international educational achievement test known as the TIMSS, which is accompanied by a 120-question survey designed to identify test takers demographically, has an uncannily exact correlation between math scores and the number of questions students are willing to answer rather than skipping.

Chapter Nine: Marita's Bargain

As we've seen, awareness of the role cultural legacies play in shaping people's destinies can help to change them (think of the turnaround of Korean Air). Another example: A public middle school program known as KIPP (Knowledge Is Power Program), which serves mostly poor African American and Hispanic kids in the Bronx, has helped students vastly surpass the area's dismal statistics on math skills. Compared to the South Bronx average of 16 percent of middle school students performing at or above their grade level in math, an unbelievable 84 percent of eighth-grade KIPP students do so.

Why? In contrast to the prevalent US educational system's belief that excessive study time is detrimental to students' well-being, KIPP lengthens the school year, with three extra weeks of classes in July. By doing so, it shrinks the "achievement gap" between well-off students who have greater access to educational activities and programs during summer vacation, and lower-income students who may enjoy their months off but aren't necessarily afforded the kind of mental stimulation that would enable them to keep academic pace with their peers. Moreover, KIPP kids have lengthy school days, with sometimes ninety minutes or more devoted to each subject. This fosters the kind of patience and willingness to work through complex problems that, as discussed in the previous chapter, facilitates achievement—and it gives kids time to absorb the lessons and connect with the material.

Twelve-year-old Marita, the daughter of a single mom, is an example of the sort of dedication that the KIPP schedule and curriculum inspire. She wakes up at 5:45 a.m. to commute to school, leaves school around 5:00 p.m., and does at least two to three hours of homework, taking a dinner break only at her mother's insistence, and going to bed between 11:00 p.m. and midnight. But this is the "bargain" referenced in the chapter title: This child wants to succeed, and is willing to log the long hours and hard work to do so.

Need to Know: An individual need not be the best and brightest to succeed—he or she need only be good enough and bright enough, willing to work hard, and have the opportunity to see one's potential nurtured.

Epilogue: A Jamaican Story

Of all of the anecdotes in *Outliers* about how fortuitous circumstances can affect one's fate, this is the most personal to the author. Gladwell's mother, Joyce, was one of twin girls born to Daisy and Donald Nation in Jamaica in 1931. When it came time to attend high school, Joyce was fortunate enough to benefit from a scholarship program instituted just years before, providing her entry into a private high school. And while her twin sister received a rare scholarship to attend university in London, Joyce did not—but her mother, Daisy, received an almost miraculous loan from a Chinese shopkeeper named, fittingly enough, Mr. Chance.

As lucky as Joyce was individually to be the beneficiary of this generosity, there was a "morally complicated" legacy that led to her being in that position in the first place. Her foremother had been purchased at a slave market by a man named William Ford, who entered into a surprisingly open relationship with her. Their descendants benefited from the privilege accorded to light-skinned people of color in Jamaica at the time. Although Gladwell's mother may not have been an "outlier" on the level of Bill Gates or the Beatles, the success she went on to achieve was similarly a product of being born into opportune circumstances and being afforded the chance to live up to her potential.

Need to Know: Though we typically view rock-star status and success as the rewards of an individual's talent, those who outperform others in their fields are invariably the beneficiaries of a complex tapestry of circumstances and opportunities. The ultimate lesson of *Outliers* may be that for every luminary who achieved greatness, things could've gone the other way—and, perhaps, the same might hold true for all those who didn't.

Cast of Characters

Joe Flom: The whip-smart, ambitious, confident son of Eastern European immigrants, he grew up in dire poverty, attended Harvard Law School, and worked his way up to being a named partner at a powerful law firm. In addition to being intelligent and driven, his success can also be attributed to being born to a hard-working father who instilled a strong work ethic in his son."

Bill Gates: The Microsoft cofounder and esteemed philanthropist is today a household name, not to mention one of the wealthiest people on the planet. He fell in love with computing as a teenager, in part due to his exposure to the technology at his school—setting him in the right place at the right time.

Bill Joy: The cofounder of Sun Microsystems is considered a highly influential Internet pioneer, instrumental in developing the UNIX and Java programming languages. His outlier status stems from his choice of college: The University of Michigan had a computer center, which became an integral part of his undergraduate life."

Christopher Langan: Hailed as possibly the smartest man in the world, with an IQ of 195, he grew up in extreme poverty, gave up on college education, and now lives on a horse farm in Missouri—while working on an expansive theory of the universe. Had the circumstances of his childhood been different, one wonders, could he have been an outlier in his field and a household name?

Daisy Nation: A schoolteacher from the Jamaican village of Harewood, she managed, despite the prohibitive costs of education, to send both of her twin daughters—one of whom would become Malcolm Gladwell's mother—to the University of London.

Robert Oppenheimer: The brilliant "father of the atomic bomb," from a privileged New York City family, landed the position of scientific director of the Manhattan Project at 38 despite relative inexperience.

Lewis Terman: A Stanford University psychology professor and the inventor of the Stanford-Binet IQ test, he studied a group of high-IQ students who came to be known as the "Termites" to track their achievements—with disappointing results.

Direct Quotes

"The culture we belong to and the legacies passed down by our forebears shape the patterns of our achievement in ways we cannot begin to imagine."

Success (or lack thereof) doesn't happen in a vacuum. Much as we may like to believe in a level playing field for all, some people are born into circumstances that are more favorable to achieving a given goal.

"Because we so profoundly personalize success, we miss opportunities to lift others onto the top rung."

Our focus on success as a product of individual achievement may blind us to the advantages that have helped others to shine, and the potential inherent in others.

"We pretend that success is exclusively a matter of individual merit."

Being gifted is not a guarantee that one will ascend to the highest ranks of a given field; hard work and the opportunity to see it rewarded are also necessary variables.

"[Lewis Terman] fell in love with the fact that his Termites were at the absolute pinnacle of the intellectual scale—at the ninety-ninth percentile of the ninety-ninth percentile of the ninety-ninth percentile—without realizing how little that seemingly extraordinary fact meant."

The psychologist's study of young geniuses through their adult lives was expected to prove that ultra-high IQs would predictably correlate with amazing accomplishments. But he was misguided in assuming that every additional IQ point on a person's score is meaningful past a certain level, and in neglecting other factors such as creativity and "practical intelligence."

"Three things—autonomy, complexity, and a connection between effort and reward—are, most people

agree, the three qualities that work has to have if it is to be satisfying."

Success comes from feeling motivated, challenged, and empowered by one's work, and being able to see the big-picture payoff for one's labors, however difficult or exhausting it might be from day to day.

"Cultural legacies are powerful forces. They have deep roots and long lives."

The attitudes and tendencies of our forebears are deeply ingrained in us, and continue to exert a strong influence on our behavior and beliefs, no matter how far removed our living conditions are from these cultural roots.

"Planes are safer when the least experienced pilot is flying, because it means the second pilot isn't going to be afraid to speak up."

Deference to authority and hierarchy may subvert a team's effective performance. When people feel comfortable communicating without a filter, they're better equipped to collaborate.

"The world could be so much richer than the world we have settled for."

Here, Gladwell is referring to a hypothetical scenario in which millions more people could take advantage of the kinds of opportunities that the outliers he has described were lucky enough to benefit from—for instance, if every 13-year-old had the same access to a computer that Bill Gates did at that age.

"The outlier, in the end, is not an outlier at all."

Those who have achieved the extraordinary are not purely in and of themselves extraordinary individuals; talented though they may be, their success is a product of multiple factors.

Trivia

1. The Beatles' first stint performing in Hamburg, Germany, in 1960, consisted of 106 gigs of five-plus hours per night.

2. Of the 75 richest people of all time—from ancient history to the present day—14 were born in America between 1831 and 1840. Number one on the list: John D. Rockefeller, born in 1839.

3. Manhattan Project mastermind Robert Oppenheimer had a rock-collecting hobby. His letters to geologists earned him a speaking engagement addressing the New York Mineralogical Club.

Only when he emerged before the audience did they discover that he was 12 years old.

4. According to Dutch psychologist Geert Hofstede's studies, the nation with the greatest level of "uncertainty avoidance"—insistence on following procedure—is Greece. The lowest-ranking—the most go-with-the-flow—country is Singapore.

5. Children in China are typically able to count to 40 at age four; for children in the United States, it's age five.

6. Malcolm Gladwell's Jamaican great-grandmother, Ann Powell, was descended from the same family as former US Secretary of State Colin Powell.

7. Is author Malcolm Gladwell an outlier? In an interview with USA Today, he attributes his success as a writer to the years he spent writing for the *Washington Post* as his 10,000 hours of practice.

What's That Word?

Accumulative advantage: The phenomenon in which possessing one advantage, even if arbitrary or circumstantial (i.e., being in the right place at the right time), leads to progressively greater advantages that can effectively create a snowball effect of success. (See also "Matthew effect.")

Achievement gap: The statistical difference in academic success between more- and less-economically advantaged students.

Analytical intelligence: The type of intellectual ability that can be measured by standardized tests such as the IQ test, it's what we typically think of when we think of what it means to be "smart"—but does not necessarily correlate with practical intelligence (see also "practical intelligence").

Matthew effect: Based on the Biblical verse Matthew 25:29 ("For unto everyone that hath shall be given, and he shall have abundance. But from him that hath not shall be taken away even that which he hath"), the Matthew effect essentially describes the principle that "the rich get richer, the poor get poorer"—in a metaphorical sense where "rich" and "poor" are defined in terms of relative advantages and disadvantages. (See also "accumulative advantage.")

Mitigated speech: A form of communication that conveys a message in an indirect or euphemistic way, requiring the receiver to "read between the lines," as it were, to grasp its true meaning.

Outlier: As used by Malcolm Gladwell, a member of a statistical sample who is far removed from the average population—one whose abilities or talents appear to be, one might say, "off the charts."

Power distance index (PDI): Coined by psychologist Geert Hofstede as one salient "dimension" of cultures, this term measures the emphasis a society places on hierarchy and differential of power.

Practical intelligence: Coined by Robert Sternberg, the term describes what we might call savvy social skills—an instinct for how to tailor our approach to different people and different circumstances in order to achieve our goals. This often unconscious knowledge does not necessarily correlate in any way with analytical intelligence.

Threshold effect: The idea that certain measurements provide advantages in certain fields—for instance, height in basketball or IQ points in academic achievement—but only up to a certain point. Past that "threshold," incremental degrees of difference don't really serve to predict relative achievement levels.

Critical Response

- A #1 *New York Times* bestseller
- A #1 *Globe and Mail* (Canada) bestseller

"After a decade—and, really, a generation—in which this country has done fairly little to build up the institutions that can foster success, Gladwell is urging us to rethink." —*The New York Times*

"Ultimately, [Gladwell] isn't trying to provide a prescription for individual success; this is not a self-help book. Rather, he seeks to focus our attention on a much more profound question: How much potential out there is being ignored? How much raw talent remains uncultivated and ultimately lost because we cling to outmoded ideas of what success looks like and what is required to achieve it?"

—*The Wall Street Journal*

"*New Yorker* writer Malcolm Gladwell explores the reason behind these strange clumps in data. His conclusion—that potential genius abounds, but little of it lands on the fertile soil of opportunity—provides a poignant theme for perhaps his most impassioned book to date." —A.V. Club

About Malcolm Gladwell

Malcolm Gladwell is known for works that offer innovative, sometimes controversial analyses of human behavior and society—often challenging our preconceived perceptions, just as *Outliers* upends common assumptions about the path to success. Gladwell picks up on details, and draws connections, that others might miss.

Born in 1963 in the United Kingdom and raised in Ontario, Canada, Gladwell is a *New Yorker* staff writer and popular podcaster who pokes and prods into phenomena we often take for granted—or aren't even cognizant of—to greatly thought-provoking effect. His breakthrough book, *The Tipping Point: How Little Things Can Make a Big Difference,* elucidated the idea of the "social epidemic," the concept that certain ideas can catch on and become "viral" much in the way that physical diseases spread. *Blink: The Power of Thinking* goes inside the human mind to analyze the dynamics of our decisions and snap judgments.

He is also the author of *What the Dog Saw: And Other Adventures* and *David and Goliath: Underdogs, Misfits, and the Art of Battling Giants,* and was named to the TIME list of the 100 most influential people in 2005.

For Your Information

Online

Author Malcolm Gladwell on His Best-selling Books."
    CBSNews.com

"Cognitive-Theoretical Model of the Universe."
    CTMU.org

"The Fourth Lesson of Joe Flom: It Has Something to
    Do With Liquidity." SuperLawers.com

"The History of the Beatles' First Hamburg Show."
    UltimateClassicRock.com

"Outliers: The Story of Success." C-SPAN.com

"Q and A With Malcolm." Gladwell.com

"The Rumpus Interview with Malcolm Gladwell."
    TheRumpus.net

"Why Malcolm Gladwell Thinks We Have Little Control Over Our Own Success." NYMag.com

Books

The 7 Habits of Highly Effective People: Powerful Lessons in Personal Change by Stephen R. Covey

The Art of Corporate Success by Ken Auletta

Biography of an Idea by Edward L. Bernays

Celebrity, Inc.: How Famous People Make Money by Jo Piazza

Chaos by James Gleick

Freakonomics by Steven D. Levitt and Stephen J. Dubner

Genius: The Life and Science of Richard Feynman by James Gleick

Grit: The Power of Passion and Perseverance by Angela Duckworth

How Children Succeed: Grit, Curiosity, and the Hidden Power of Character by Paul Tough

How Successful People Think: Change Your Thinking, Change Your Life by John C. Maxwell

Mindset: The New Pyschology of Success by Carol S. Dweck

On Being Human by Erich Fromm

Peak: Secrets from the New Science of Expertise by Anders Ericsson and Robert Pool

A Student's Guide to Economics by Paul Heyne

Writers in America by Budd Schulberg

Other Books by Malcolm Gladwell

Blink: The Power of Thinking Without Thinking

David and Goliath: Underdogs, Misfits, and the Art of Battling Giants

The Tipping Point: How Little Things Can Make a Big Difference

What the Dog Saw: And Other Adventures

Bibliography

Donahue, Deirdre. "Malcolm Gladwell's 'Success' defines 'Outlier' achievement." *USA Today.* http://usatoday30.usatoday.com/life/books/news/2008-11-17-gladwell-success_N.htm.

Gladwell, Malcolm. *Outliers: The Story of Success.* New York: Back Bay Books, 2011.

Outlier. Dictionary.com Unabridged. Random House, Inc. http://www.dictionary.com/browse/outlier. Accessed: October 29, 2016.

WORTH BOOKS
SMART SUMMARIES

So much to read,
so little time?

Explore summaries of bestselling
fiction and essential nonfiction
books on a variety of subjects,
including business, history, science,
lifestyle, and much more.

Visit the store at
www.ebookstore.worthbooks.com

MORE SMART SUMMARIES
FROM WORTH BOOKS

POPULAR SCIENCE

WORTH BOOKS
SMART SUMMARIES
Summary and
Analysis of
THE GENE
An Intimate History

Based on the Book by
Siddhartha Mukherjee

WORTH BOOKS
SMART SUMMARIES
Summary and
Analysis of
HIDDEN FIGURES
The American Dream and the
Untold Story of the Black Women
Mathematicians Who Helped
Win the Space Race

Based on
the Book
by Margot
Lee Shetterly

WORTH BOOKS
SMART SUMMARIES
Summary and
Analysis of
**THE HIDDEN
LIFE OF TREES**
What They Feel, How They
Communicate—Discoveries
from a Secret World

Based on the Book
by Peter Wohlleben

WORTH BOOKS
SMART SUMMARIES
Summary and
Analysis of
**THE IMMORTAL
LIFE OF
HENRIETTA
LACKS**

Based on
the book
by Rebecca
Skloot

WORTH BOOKS
SMART SUMMARIES
Summary and
Analysis of
OUTLIERS
The Story of Success

Based on the Book by
Malcolm Gladwell

WORTH BOOKS
SMART SUMMARIES
Summary and
Analysis of
SAPIENS
A Brief History
of Humankind

Based on
the Book
by Yuval
Noah
Harari

WORTH BOOKS
SMART SUMMARIES
Summary and
Analysis of
STIFF
The Curious Lives
of Human Cadavers

Based on the Book
by Mary Roach

WORTH BOOKS
SMART SUMMARIES
Summary and
Analysis of
**THINKING,
FAST AND
SLOW**

Based on
the Book
by Daniel
Kahneman

WORTH BOOKS
SMART SUMMARIES

MORE SMART SUMMARIES
FROM WORTH BOOKS

BUSINESS

WORTH BOOKS
SMART SUMMARIES